EARTH GIANT TREE GIFT SERIES – BOOK 7

Snow Gum's Gift

ROCHELLE HEVEREN

 TREE VOICE PUBLISHING

Earth Giant Tree Gift Series: Snow Gum's Gift

TREE VOICE PUBLISHING PTY LTD
ACN. 627 784 294 ABN . 94627784294
4 Wirreanda Court Blackburn Victoria 3130 AUSTRALIA
Phone +613 9878 4600
Email: hello@treevoice.global
www.treevoice.global

First published in 2019
Copyright text © Rochelle Heveren
Copyright © Tree Voice Publishing

www.facebook.com/TreeVoiceAuthor
www.facebook.com/RochelleHeverenAuthor
Instagram: @treevoiceglobal
Instagram: @rochelle_with_love_x

All rights reserved. No part of this publication may be reproduced in whole or in part, stored in a retrievable system, or transmitted in any form or by any means, electronic, mechanical, photocopying, recording or otherwise, without written permission of the copyright holder or publisher.

Designed by Tree Voice Publishing Pty Ltd
Printed by Ingram Spark
ISBN: 978-0-6483912-9-6 (paperback)

 A catalogue record for this book is available from the National Library of Australia

*I know with my whole being,
that when I sit and a tree connects,
that it is never just for me.*

*This little book
has BIG heart and soul.*

*My commitment to share this with you,
my friend, is promised.*

– Love Rochelle xxx

I feel pounding in my chest and my whole body tingles as I walk up to the ancient snow gum at the top of the High Country in Victoria, Australia.

The extremes in environment and weather have gifted Snow Gum with many visible characteristics that make him unique. I learn to live, embracing my own uniqueness. With my own inner peace and self-nurture I learn that any external storm can be endured. My own perception is vital in living my life full of happiness.

Foreword

Snow Gum's Gift is the channelled teachings of one of Earth's great Masters. This wise being, over thousands of years, will bring you calm, strength, motivation and peace and a unique way of guiding life's journey, reminding you of the importance of your own inner calm in all areas of your life. You will discover that the way you perceive your life determines your journey. Snow Gum will remind you of the importance of observing the details of life around you, as a way of being present. You will learn that the cocoon of life's restrictions can be broken to allow freedom to really live if you send your own self-love to any part of you needing nurture. Experience deep calm, stillness and love while connecting into Snow Gum.

Being supported with the magic of *Snow Gum's Gift* is like climbing up into the centre of his massive trunk. It is like resting your body on one of his many branches and listening to his whispers of great wisdom.
Allow his words to encourage you with love.

This inspiring gift book is designed to unlock your own heart's wisdom. Rochelle invites you to discover the magic, stillness and newfound freedom that she experienced, sitting and resting her back against the Snow Gum up in the High Country in Mansfield, Australia.

Written in Mansfield, Australia

Contents

Introduction 1

Chapter 1: Make a Wish 6

Chapter 2: Giving Away and Trust 11

Chapter 3: Uniqueness 15

Chapter 4: Loss 18

Chapter 5: Being Present 23

Chapter 6: Support 28

Chapter 7: Choice 33

Chapter 8: Gifted Love 36

Chapter 9: Safety 40

Chapter 10: Self-Love 45

Chapter 11: Perception 48

Introduction

I meet a snow gum on my journey back from Sydney. Michael and I have decided to detour six hours to the top of the highest peak in Australia, a mount called Kosciuszko. We park our car at the foot of a fairly steep hill to make our way toward the top, tiptoing across marshes that were wet from the melted snow. It is difficult to prevent my shoes from being engulfed in the soggy earth. Clear ice-cold water runs in the surrounding creeks, once snow.

As I make my way toward the top of the mountain I have to push myself through thick bush that stands nearly at my height. There are several boulders that I have to climb over or around. My focus is on the tree at the top. I can see the tips of a magnificent snow gum. When I finally arrive up at this tree, towering above me, I open my heart into its essence.

When I am told that through this tree I will learn

about obstacles, I roll my eyes. Great, that is all I need! I wonder why I have walked up all that way, experiencing obstacles at every step, to connect into this essence.

I sit for a short while, not saying anything. My thoughts are interrupted by a reassurance that the essence of Snow Gum can help me overcome obstacles. My attention is spiked!

It is interesting that I have worked with some difficulty to reach the top of this hill to meet this tree. I have already endured obstacles in order to stand beside Snow Gum. After my initial rejection of the idea of facing and overcoming obstacles, I remember that everything happens for a reason and perhaps I have some clearing to do in my life.

After a short while enjoying the peace and solitude of Kosciuszko at the end of the snow season, Michael and I decide to head back to our vehicle to continue our long journey home.

Then the strangest thing happens.

For the next couple of weeks uncomfortable and inconvenient events keep happening. I go to get my hair coloured but return home with jet black hair instead of my usual brown. I have to face the embarrassment of calling my hairdresser to tell her of her mistake. She invites me back so she can fix the error.

Whilst out on the lake with friends I try to steer our houseboat and take a phone call, at the same time as tying a jet ski onto the back of our boat. My mobile phone slips and falls, disappearing to the bottom of the lake. I watch it all happen as if in slow motion! Not everything has been backed up on my phone, so much of my data is lost forever. It is extremely frustrating to have to start again with a new phone.

To my surprise though, whilst these and other obstacles are arising, I discover a burning desire to get things sorted. I feel motivated to release anything negative in my life.

I host a stand at a *Mind Body Spirit* Festival in my home town of Melbourne, where I meet a young girl who takes groups of people on walks and expeditions in the High Country of Victoria. She tells me that she knows of the most magnificent snow gum up in between two mountain peaks called King Billy 1 and King Billy 2. She has taken a group of 30 young girls up to this amazing snow gum – they all climbed up and sat on the branches of this massive ancient tree! I tell her about the snow gum that I have recently connected with on Mount Kosciuszko and all the obstacles I have experienced since then. I also share that my sense of motivation has not been this high for a very long time. We laugh as we share stories. When she shows me a photo of her snow gum, I shiver with excitement. I know that I have to visit this snow gum.

Several weeks later, while up at our farm, Michael asks if I would like him to take me to the top of the High Country to find the snow gum I've told him about, the one that sits between the two mountain peaks. Michael also has a passion for adventure and loves exploring the outdoors. I am excited by his offer. One of my sons is kind enough to lend us his four-wheel drive and, in an instant, Michael begins to load it up. It takes three hours to get to the peak so we decide to take a few extra supplies just in case we get stuck – plenty of water, a couple of cans of spaghetti, a four-wheel drive winch (that I hope we don't have to use) and a swag to sleep in overnight.

Up to the High Country we go.

As we drive up into the High Country toward this ancient snow gum, I am curious to see whether I will feel the same sense of essence I felt with the other snow gum.

For the past few days it has rained so much that there has been flash-flooding in some of the surrounding country towns. Even the city of Melbourne has experienced water damage. Because we are heading to the High Country, I'm fairly confident we should be fine. In the back of my mind however, I am feeling cautious, given all the mishaps that arose after I met the other snow gum.

I have to trust that all will be fine.

I haven't been four-wheel driving in many years. I bounce around in the passenger seat. It seems I'm not as fond of four-wheel driving as I remember being years ago!

CHAPTER 1

Make a Wish

When we reach the ridge called the Bluff Track, there are so many snow gum trees that I wonder how I will know which is the one the girl has told me about.

Then I feel my chest pounding and my body tingling. This snow gum's energy is so powerful! Along with the altitude up here in the High Country, it makes me feel a little giddy.

Unmistakably the ancient snow gum stands out. He is larger than all the other snow gums here. His presence is unlike any other tree that I have met before. I walk directly up to him and instantly feel welcomed to not just stand beside him, but right in the centre of his massive trunk branching out in all directions.

"Finally, we meet," I say.

"I hope your journey has helped muster excitement in you." His gentle strong voice penetrates through me.

"Yes, although I felt very bounced about in our car, I also felt great excitement, not only for my adventure but also a sense of motivation to reach the top and stand with you," I reply.

"Sit yourself down and get comfortable," Snow Gum invites me.

I instantly feel my shoulders relax. My body wants to slump into the full embrace of Snow Gum.

"I notice every one of your branches is very different from the others. I imagine every branch holds a gift or lesson," I observe.

"Just think – all this has grown from one tiny seed! My twists and turns hold a mirror to your own life, my friend."

I find we have already connected – I do not need my usual three breaths to forge a connection.

"Well, yes, for sure. My life has taken many turns, this way and that. I have an abundance of things that

I've learned along the way."

I realise I am speaking very fast from excitement, so I try to slow myself down by pausing. Then I say, "I cannot help but notice that you are still pushing out new growth in clumps here and there from your trunk and branches."

"One never stops growing, learning and expanding. Notice I am solid, strong and interesting." Snow Gum laughs as he says the word 'interesting'.

"You are very interesting – not only to look at; I also feel elated sitting in your presence. I feel you are holding me in a beautiful embrace. I feel lighter. In fact, I feel that nothing can stand in my way if I really want something badly enough," I state.

"I know you seek my gifts to then share them with others. My first gift today is this feeling you are already soaking up. It's the feeling that you can do anything," Snow Gum tells me.

"I like that. Wow, anything!... So, the sky's the limit?" I ask.

"There is no limit, my friend. You just need to wish it and then commit to it at any cost. I saw you stop at the dandelions over there. Did you ever pick these as a child and make a wish?"

I smile. I spotted these flowering weeds growing everywhere on the side of the road as we drove up here as well. I say, "Yes, they all caught my eye."

"Well, I am a tree who can grant a wish. If you could have anything you want right now, what would that be?" he invites me to consider.

I sit silently for a few minutes. I smile, knowing that Snow Gum is like my very own genie tree.

"I wish that all physical pain would be gone from my body. I want flexibility back, with fluid joints and mobility," I wish aloud. "Oh, and one other thing – can I please be completely present to my body? What I mean by this is that I want to feel fully."

"It is done, my friend. You shall move with ease and flexibility. You will support this movement with clean living. To achieve this, you will need to walk every single day. You need to move. Without growth and movement, you seize up," Snow Gum tells me. "If I didn't move and grow, the same thing would happen to me. Also, when you are experiencing any blockage or restriction in your body, physically or emotionally, all you need to do is breathe into your heart and send your heart's energy there. This is how you have connected to me. Now it's time for you to connect into your own body in the same way. Notice what happens."

Snow Gum will grant my wish, but I also have my own part to play as well.

"Thank you... I feel motivated to give it all a go," I say.

I hear many birds in chorus as the sun finally shines through the storm clouds above my head. The rain only stopped just before we arrived. All around me are bursting bouquets of wild flowers. I hear wind in the trees below. Up where I sit, it's surprisingly calm. I feel centred and at peace.

"You are worth the journey. Thank you. I feel inspired, held and encouraged."

"Stay for a while. I'd like to share more with you," Snow Gum invites me.

So, I do.

CHAPTER 2

Giving Away and Trust

I move onto another of Snow Gum's branches that is up slightly higher. I comfortably roll onto my stomach. I imagine it must look funny for anyone to see me slumped like this across Snow Gum's branch. But Michael has gone for a walk and I am the only one here with my new friend. I rest my head onto the branch and instantly feel restful, still and held.

"Thank you for supporting me," I say quietly. I can still feel so much of Snow Gum's strength infusing right through me.

"You're welcome. Thank you for hanging around. I want to now share that it is safe for you to trust. You have a huge struggle with trust. You need to know that if you cannot trust, then it limits enriched engagement."

I know what he is talking about. I have often found myself trusting the wrong people. They have ended up being around me only for their own self-gain. They wanted to take something from me. I wonder why I have attracted these people into my life.

As if he hears my thoughts, Snow Gum continues: "It's time you stopped giving yourself away. You have given, because your kind spirit prompts you to do so. But takers always come running when they see generosity. Stop giving to please, to fit in or to receive friendship. People worthy of your trust will never expect anything from you other than friendship, love and time together."

He is right. By giving myself away, I'm often disappointed when inevitably it doesn't achieve what I'm looking for anyway. Over time I end up becoming suspicious of most people. This is perhaps something that I have set in motion in the first place. When I've been overly generous, people have taken, then as soon as I've stopped giving, they've disappeared and I've become disappointed that they are no longer in my life.

"How do I shift this? How is this connected to trust?" I seek further clarity.

"You must check to see if you are giving, just to get an outcome."

My mind instantly turns to the gifts I've given some of my mentors and teachers over the years. Perhaps I wanted them to really like me. Instead, they took the liberty of manipulating me. All I ended up gaining was a feeling of having been taken advantage of, not the respect I craved. I have felt very hurt by this.

"Gifts are a very special thing. Never give without careful consideration. I am only gifting you now because I know you will treasure, honour and share what you are given," Snow Gum confides.

As I lay on this branch of my friend, I think I understand this lesson and gift. It is time to stop giving myself away. I need to honour myself, my time and love, giving only to those who have no ulterior motive.

Before I move to the next branch I forgive myself for having given to the wrong people. I also forgive myself for having given to get things back in return – things like friendship and the affirmation of others. I promise myself that I will begin to trust people more. Perhaps I've just been looking in all the wrong places.

I lift my body off Snow Gum and notice there are massive growths, burls, on the sides of his branch. The tip of this branch reaches very high. I notice incredible twists and turns.

"Thank you."

I feel my awareness shift. I've not known before now that my instinct to give myself away has ended up eroding my ability to trust others genuinely.

"My heart thanks you," I say, before I shift to a new place within Snow Gum.

CHAPTER 3

Uniqueness

I shift my position toward the next large branch. Three metres further out and up on this branch, I can see several branches spreading in different directions. They look like hands and fingers, all clasping each another.

"I can't help but notice the mass directional changes here on this branch. What happened?" I ask.

"Environment, weather and the need to stay secure caused this."

"Is there a gift or lesson you have about environment?" I ask.

"Indeed, you are twisted and turned. You learn this way or that. You change your mind and sometimes sit in confusion. This is the confusion caused by outside influence," Snow Gum begins to explain.

I nod. My own life has shifted and challenged me toward new ways of being. I have made decisions, only to then change my mind. I notice that there isn't a sign of 'give up' in my friend. Instead I notice that there's just a shift and turn... a yearning for something more.

"I find this branch the most interesting," I tell my friend.

"Just as I find you. The unique way you have navigated through your life makes you irresistible. I am also curious about how you have been altered by your environment. I love seeing how you have adapted and grown," Snow Gum reflects back.

Wow, if I look like this branch to Snow Gum, then he's sure to find me fascinating!

"It takes strength and determination to not give up. You have always found a way of adapting in order to survive, even in the harshest of conditions," Snow Gum explains what he sees.

I know what he's referring to: my broken childhood and my ability to remove and shut down parts of myself emotionally, physically and mentally in order to survive. I even blocked out the pain I should have naturally felt during the birth of my sons. I have forced myself to be 'happy' at times during my life, when all I wanted was to numb out and disappear. My friend Snow Gum sees me as clearly as I see him.

"Know that you are unique and stunning because of all you have endured. I find you as beautiful as you find me," Snow Gum says.

"Thank you."

No more words are needed. I feel reassured that my own uniqueness is what makes me special and unique. Right now, I do feel comfort in my own uniqueness and pride in the multi-faceted journey that has brought me to this point.

This is what makes me, 'me'. What a valuable lesson!

CHAPTER 4

Loss

I lower myself around and onto the next branch that shoots off Snow Gum's main trunk and sit with one leg on either side. My legs hang relaxed. I imagine again that I must look funny to anyone who might see me. I cannot see Michael and presume he is still wandering around the area.

This branch butts in at the base to join another, providing me a comfortable back-rest. This part of Snow Gum looks dead. It is fully grey and dry, not multi-coloured like the rest of my friend. The branch is covered in lichen. When I look at this branch, I instantly feel a deep sense of sadness – this is a branch of loss.

"You guessed correctly. In life, there is always loss. Sometimes loved ones, friendships, and that which should have been, die."

My friend pauses before continuing: "I see that your victory this past week stirs up not only happiness but also sadness in your heart."

Tears well up, as I hang my head. I had committed myself to striving for justice in response to all the sexual abuse to which I was subjected by my brother. My father also took from me. About eight years ago, my father died and I lost the opportunity to seek justice for his actions. In many ways I know my brother is also dead within, even though his body is still alive. Along with my father, my brother murdered something within me. I was taken from and broken. As a young girl, I was suffocated. Tears roll down my now adult cheeks. I grieve not only my own loss of self. Even though my brother is in jail, I feel sadness over the loss of what should have been a loving family.

"I should have been loved, held with care, nurtured and supported. I feel enormous loss for what didn't thrive and live abundantly within my life." I look out to the far-reaching tips of Snow Gum's massive branch.

"On the inside, I still live, just as you do. This branch is not dead – just as events in your life didn't kill you either. You changed, but you are still here, just as I am. You achieved this massive victory after so many years. You have achieved a completion, a break in the cycle to the sexual, physical and emotional abuse, for many future generations. Remember that not everyone is as strong as you are. Remember the many obstacles, the blocks around your voice, the emotionally shut-down way you have been in order to survive. This is no longer. You're no longer trapped, your life no longer needs to be on hold."

Then he changes the subject slightly: "Right now it's butterfly time – have you noticed them dancing?"

I had noticed this. "Yes, I saw butterflies everywhere at the farm yesterday." I smile. I know that Snow Gum is trying to lighten my mood.

"Within the confines of a cocoon, the caterpillar waits with patience, self-nurture and determination. Eventually the cocoon cracks open, light shines in and the caterpillar is changed. Then emerges a stunning butterfly! Freedom is granted. You are just like the butterfly, Rochelle. Now is the time for you to crack out of what has held you in. It's time to spread your wings and fly!"

I breathe in the fresh mountain air. I am free and I cannot go back inside that cocoon now that it has been cracked open.

"What is the link between this branch and the butterfly?" I ask.

"The centre of something holds its essence. The centre of this branch that you have seen as lifeless, is in fact still alive. You think that parts of you are dead and lost. They're not – they just need to be loved, nurtured and revived back into being. You are not a loss. When you can love all parts of yourself, you will be just like the butterfly that has been held – restrained – by its cocoon. Please notice that my seemingly dead branch actually gives me balance because I have never given up on pouring energy into it. Every part of me is special and loved," Snow Gum says with tenderness.

"Thank you for your truth and for giving me a different view of what I have always thought was dead. I have felt pain over my own emotional, physical and mental limits. I have also felt loss over the people who have let me down. I now understand that I can nurture myself with love, to revive myself and finally become free," I whisper.

As if nature has also heard our conversation, I watch nearby butterflies dancing around my friend Snow Gum, and around the many wild flowers growing in this area. All of these butterflies were held in a cocoon until they were finally ready to be set free. Deep within, they prepared for their release... and now they dance and fly freely!

I must not focus on what held me. It's time to crack open the cocoon and fly free.

I jump down from Snow Gum's branches as I hear Michael calling out, asking if I want to set up camp for the night. I happily agree. Although rain is hanging in the air, I'm not yet ready to leave my new friend and the way he makes me feel when I am around him.

CHAPTER 5

Being Present

I jump into our car and we drive up to a ledge just up from where Snow Gum stands. We notice a couple of old circular rocked fireplaces in this area – remnants of the campsites of others who have been here before us. Gathering twigs and discarded dry wood, together Michael and I build a fire in one of the stone pits. Neither of us can find matches or a lighter in the car. Just before Michael sets about rubbing sticks together to try to spark a flame, we are both excited when I find a cigarette lighter tucked inside the back seat of my son's car. Before long we are sitting beside a roaring fire. It isn't really cold but we know that later tonight the temperature will drop.

Michael chooses where the canopy and swag can be set up to keep us out of the inclement weather.

We are perched up on a ledge with views on both sides.

Once I know camp is set, I leave Michael there and head back to spend precious time with my new friend, Snow Gum.

Instantly I feel my energy shift when Snow Gum returns to view.

I've been slowly making my way around his many branches during my time connecting with him, so I decide to return to where I've left off.

Thick bark encases the next branch, unlike the other branches which are mostly bare. The bark clings to the branch, wrapped around in a circular form. On most trees, the bark is usually vertical. It's different with my friend Snow Gum here.

"I'm back!" I announce.

All is still. A quietness has hushed this area. Right now, I cannot hear the birds as I did earlier. Then, after a few minutes, one bird calls out. The wind returns to play once more in the leaves of the surrounding trees. It sounds like an orchestra, full of many musical instruments.

"Shhh... just sit and observe," I'm encouraged.

I notice many ants of all sizes scurrying around and over Snow Gum. I also see tiny butterflies, even smaller than those I saw earlier. This makes me smile as I recall our last conversation of being cocooned and then free – they are still flying free! Underneath a sheet of bark, I see patterns that look like artwork etched in the wood of the branch. Shades of grey bark, graded from light to dark, encircle all of my friend. I notice the dead parts growing lichen, as well as the smooth bare colourful limbs.

My thoughts are interrupted as Snow Gum begins to speak.

"My next gift is about being present in this very moment. Did you notice your heart beating more slowly when you became observant? Your mind-chatter was also gone. Your ability to really take notice allows space for you to simply be. There's no rushing or escaping what is happening in front of you right now. One of the most important activities you can gift yourself is being still and present," Snow Gum shares.

He is right. I feel calm, peaceful and centred. I hear the odd bird call out. This time, though, it's not just a background noise. I listen and also feel every bird's song. I find it interesting that this gift of presence is highlighted by the branch that still needs to shed its bark. It's like it's slower than all the other branches; it's not in a hurry.

I continue my focus on the many details of Snow Gum. He is abundant with difference. I sit for a long time in the gift of being present to the 'now'. I feel in no hurry and am rejuvenated by this simple act, rather than feeling drained and drawn away to another time and place.

"Whenever you feel tired, exhausted or flustered, please remember this moment. All you need to do is be present to the intricate details of life. When you do this your heart will settle instantly, as well as your mind."

"Thank you, I will," I promise.

I'm in no hurry to break the magic of this gift and lesson. I hear the different birds singing their own unique chorus. I watch insects busying themselves. The breeze moves the leaves of my friend as well as my own hair. Then my focus shifts to my body surface. My skin and fine hairs respond to my surroundings. My breath enters my nose and is released the same way. I blink my eyes. The corners of my mouth turn up as I smile.

My thoughts are uncluttered. What a gift to really be present to right now! I close my eyes for a while to soak in my heightened feelings. I feel restful and contented.

I could easily go lie in my swag with Michael right now, but decide instead to shift branches.

CHAPTER 6

Support

Around I move, and onto the following branch of my friend. Instantly I feel woken from the blissful space I've just experienced.

I notice that there's a new tree growing from the base of the trunk beneath this branch. I know that it's only possible for this baby tree to come into being because of the nutrients being fed from Snow Gum. I look out to the whole area around this oldest snow gum and wonder whether all the trees come from my friend.

"There are so many snow gums all around you here. Are they all from you?" I ask.

"So many are my offspring. My root system travels a very long way. But I'm not the only elder here in this grove. There are several other trees that reach out and seed new beginnings."

As far as I can see, I witness the mass of snow gums in this community. I notice that there aren't any other tree species up here in the Highlands of Victoria.

"Why are there only snow gums growing here?" I ask.

"Wind, rain, storms, snow, fires and harsh conditions make it impossible for many other tree species, especially trees that are delicate." Snow Gum sounds proud to share.

"Most snow gum trees are not tall, but rather short, solid and outstretched. Twists and turns constitute their beauty. Their secret is their ability to endure so much and still survive."

"I feel your strength. I also feel the strength of your community. Your family holds hands beneath the earth," I comment.

"You have tapped into our strength. Together, united, we can endure extremes. When you are alone, it's easier to give up. Remember back to your recent victory – you didn't achieve this alone."

He is right. I helped others who had also been

victimised by my brother. I wasn't alone and together we supported and encouraged each other, and didn't give up. I feel a tight bond with every one of these people. I smile. Working on a cause with others is a gift.

"I suspect this 'gift' you are describing, is support – supporting others and also being supported. Belonging is a very special thing," I confirm.

"If any trees in my family grove are unwell, we all send them what they need. I've also received from them at times," Snow Gum tells me.

The natural phenomenon of trees helping each other is beautiful.

Resting my back, I feel love and care, and wonder what new gift Snow Gum is sending me.

I move again, sitting right in Snow Gum's centre. There are a couple of metres of cleared space at the top of his trunk. It isn't far up from the ground. Here I feel most comfortable, perhaps because I am sitting in his heart centre.

"I believe you are named after the mountain here that has two peaks, King Billy 1 and King Billy 2," I comment.

"I am the centre, the heart, you might say. Yes, that's how I am named, and I like it. People come up here sometimes just to see me. I feel special knowing people have gone to an effort. It's the key ingredient for success – the effort, that is." Snow Gum Billy shares.

"If someone goes to an effort, it makes others feel special," I repeat.

"Yes, it is the ultimate gift for someone to go to a special effort. Like your husband today – he had so much he could have been doing back at your farm but he loves you enough to prioritise your wish to come and visit me."

"I know how special that is – I've felt so much love today. Michael has wanted to camp for years. He also loves four-wheel driving, but I haven't been keen for either thing in such a long time. I guess I've been stuck in the rut of my life. Michael, on the other hand, always looks for ways to show love." I feel a little guilty that I don't do enough to show my love in a similar way.

My thoughts then take me to those of us who have recently celebrated our victory in finding justice. By supporting each another, we have shown love and care.

I decide that from today I will find ways to make others feel loved and valued. I know how good it makes me feel and I wish to be the one responsible for helping others feel this way also. Michael has no agenda other than to see me happy. I soak in the love all around me and wonder how he's going up by our campfire.

CHAPTER 7

Choice

The next branch looks like a set of twins. They start as one branch then divide out into different directions. This is the twin-branch.

"What can you share about the branch that I see as two?" I ask.

"There is always a choice in life: to go one way or another. Some things are meant to divide – ideas, thoughts, wishes and journeys can take us in different directions. This dual branch is a reminder that you always have a choice. No one is forced to decide one way over another," Snow Gum Billy announces.

I know that whenever I consider anything, I try to weigh up several things, even if only the pros and cons of the situation.

"Take a look at the outer tips of these twin branches and tell me what you notice," Billy asks.

I immediately notice that the outer tip of both branches reaches the same height. Both branches certainly twist and turn and become thick and thin in different places along the branch but, in the end, they arrive at the same place.

"They arrive at the same place, but they have grown very differently," I observe.

"It can take longer sometimes, depending on the direction you choose. You may endure more events – or adventures as I call them – in choosing one direction over another. Just know that there is never really a shortcut. The same goal can be achieved in more than one way. What's important is what's achieved in the end, not which way you choose to take to get there," Snow Gum Billy teaches me.

I consider this. It is plain and simple as I observe that the journey of two different branches have ended up with them reaching the same place. They have both grown out and reached up. I find this idea not only fascinating but comforting. Sometimes I spend way too much time stressing over choosing the 'correct' way to go. Yet perhaps what's more important is the action of striving toward my goal.

"Thank you for taking that pressure away," I say to my friend.

From now on, I'm going to wish, dream and strive, without wasting too much time over the 'how'. I will be guided by my own choices and by what feels right at the time.

I know it's not only the pressure that Snow Gum Billy is taking away from my future choices. It's also the confusion I find myself experiencing whenever I have to decide which way is 'correct'. At times I know that this confusion has made me walk away from making any choice at all. Now I think of all the lost opportunities for growth.

I guess my new lesson and gift is to make a choice, and then do it.

CHAPTER 8

Gifted Love

I walk back up to our campsite and notice many more dandelions, all puffy and ready to be plucked and blown into the air along with a wish. I choose a nice big one, and with one big breath I set all the little seeds with fluffy parachutes free, to softly settle wherever they will then grow.

Camp looks so homely. Our swag sits under a canopy, holding a mattress and sleeping bags. Our cooler bag has chilled wine, which Michael offers me. He is in full camping mode and cooking the first round of dinner tonight. He has slightly opened a tin of spaghetti and sat it to heat in the open fire. This whole scene is basic, but romance hangs sweetly in the air. After a small feed and a glass of wine, Michael takes me by the hand. He asks if I'd like to see some of the other trees in the area he'd noticed while I was connecting to Snow Gum.

Down on the opposite ledge, the trees are not as wide but they are taller. There's one tree that looks twisted the whole way up its trunk. This place is magical and we both enjoy the calm. We look at tree after tree and share our observations with each other. It's nice to do this with Michael.

Eventually we head back to our campsite on the ridge above Snow Gum. After a short while sitting by the fire I sense that night is not too far off, so I decide to go and connect once more to Snow Gum Billy.

"I think we are the only ones up here for the night. There hasn't been a car pass all afternoon," I comment.

"You are so privileged to have this area to yourselves. Often this area can be very busy with visitors. Have you decided to spend the night?" Snow Gum Billy asks.

"I'm scared to break the spell you have cast over me. Of all the places Michael and I could be, it is in your home I feel the need to be right now," I confess.

Regardless of what weather will come, I want to

trust that here, right now, we are re-charging our own 'human batteries'. This week held the gift of justice and a conclusion to a long ordeal, but it also overloaded my senses with emotion. Now I need to settle and recover.

"Can you tell me what your favourite gift is? What is the one thing you love to do with people who stop to admire you?" I ask.

"It always depends on who visits. But I do like to connect with someone who feels lost, as well as with those who feel alone. They may be involved with many people in their lives but still feel lost. I love to give them a feeling of being loved," Snow Gum Billy tells me.

I know exactly what he is talking about. I too felt instant connection and love as soon as I rested on and around this Snow Gum. I don't feel lost right now. This beautiful boost of unconditional love is amazing. I guess that's why I don't want to leave.

"I have felt your love, thank you. I'm in no rush to leave. As I sleep near you tonight, please show me one final gift or lesson," I ask.

I know he's done so much already but I don't always get to stay and sleep so close to a tree I've connected with, particularly through the night.

"Your wish, my friend, I will grant with pleasure." Billy gives me his word.

I place my hand onto him and bid him goodnight.

I wander back to the crackling fire. It's warm and the last of today's sun shines bright. The grey sky that was present when we arrived has shifted from dark grey to white, and is now a vibrant blue. This feels like a magical paradise. I wonder why I have waited so long to camp and spend time in nature.

CHAPTER 9

Safety

The final moments of the late afternoon continue to be magical. Our fire warms me as well as invoking a meditative state. In this moment, I embrace all that is. Birds of all varieties sing out their last day's chorus. After our next can of spaghetti for dinner is cooked on the open fire, I think about how much fuss I often put into preparing a meal. Not tonight, it took just minutes.

The last rays of sun are warm. The sun sends shards of light through the clouds, setting a vibrant gold hue. Finally, the sun also turns in for the night.

Rain has been forecast, so we make sure the canopy over our swag is secured. When all is quiet, our fire is distinguished with puddle water and we get into our swag and zip ourselves in.

We generate enough body heat to feel warm and comfortable, and I drift off to sleep. Occasionally I wake when I hear the wind starting down in the gully, then gaining force when it hits our site. Our windy night very soon escalates into a full-blown storm. The light sprinkle of rain thrashes and all at once heavy constant rain is upon us. There is wind, rain and beating weather outside, yet within I feel calm.

I drift back to sleep, contained and safe. I hear the refrain of Snow Gum Billy from up the hill, reassuring me that it's OK and I am safe. He tells me I am protected by all the snow gum essence that covers this whole area. I roll over and snuggle in. I feel strong, anchored and able to withstand the storm.

Then Snow Gum Billy takes me on his promised journey. I'm taken through the four seasons and all the elements that the snow gums up here experience. I experience the scorching heat in summer when the twigs and leaves dry; the storms and heavy downpour in winter; and the strength of the wind in autumn. No wonder my friend's outer branches have been twisted in all directions. Then I see the blanket of snow that freezes this whole area. I feel the energy within Snow Gum settling. It's hibernation time. My dream takes me though all my emotions, knowing that my endurance strengthens me to feel safe. I feel protected internally, even though things are wild externally.

I wake up fully and struggle to breathe. I feel desperate for fresh air so I open up part of the swag and poke my head out. I wonder if this is how the butterfly feels moments before it finally breaks free.

The rain has stopped but the wind is still forceful. In the distance lightning illuminates the sky. As soon as Michael sees the lightning, he decides it is time for us to go. I am torn between continuing to endure the storm and agreeing to leave. I remember Snow Gum Billy's words about choice and know that I will end up at the same spot in the end. Perhaps my lesson and gift will be accomplished regardless. Even though I feel keen to stay in my safe and protected state, I feel happy to follow Michael's lead. While the rain takes a breather, we pack everything into the back of our four-wheel drive.

Within 15 minutes of leaving our camp, the sun begins to lighten the sky. I welcome the sunshine through my open car window, and also hear the birds awaken.

What an adventure!

The whole time, I have felt safe. I think about the contrast between the cocoon of my swag and the chaos of the wild weather outside. This is exactly how life can be at times. It takes endurance and dedication to feel calm and safe, regardless.

In my life these contrasts have been extreme. At times I've gone out to play in the storm, like a child splashing in puddles. Then I've been thrown and tossed about, and left feeling exhausted. At other times I've been strong and resilient, just like the snow gum. I haven't felt caught up in external dramas as I've been focussed on my mission.

My heart thanks Snow Gum Billy for reminding me that everything involves a choice. I remember the twin branches that both finished up in the same place in the end.

My inner world is crucial to me remaining calm so that I can endure any external storm. In the end, it's always going to be my choice.

Today I feel present and I observe every detail we pass through my car window: vibrant flowers and bouncing rabbits, kangaroo and deer. Everything anchors me into this time of 'now'.

My heart-thread is still connected to my friend Snow Gum Billy.

CHAPTER 10

Self-Love

I find a quiet moment the next day to go and sit by my new friend in a visionary spiritual space. My initial visit and threading to Snow Gum Billy enables me to do this even though we are no longer in physical proximity.

Sitting in his heart centre, I breathe into my heart three times, my hand on one of his many branches.

"Thank you for showing me through the night what it feels like to be you. I was enlightened to see the extremes between my own inner and outer world. You showed me that my inner core strength is vital in withstanding any external storm," I say.

"Staying focussed and committed is only possible when you love yourself fully. Every limb, twig, leaf, gumnut and earth root is vital to my own survival.

You, my friend, are no different," Snow Gum Billy shares.

"Are you telling me that at the core of your strength and commitment to endure extremes is the ability to live through every part of you?" I check to ensure I've understood correctly.

"It is beneficial. I send my essence to every part of myself. I love my own uniqueness. There are no two trees the same, just like humans. Yet I see humans constantly trying to be like others. This is impossible and some people lose purpose as a result – I see this when they come to sit with me. They despise who they are and forget how to gain strength from loving every single part of themselves."

Billy pauses, then continues. "I saw your freedom last night with your husband. You embraced and loved yourself fully first. I witnessed you sending freedom to your whole body. This allowed you to love another person."

I blush slightly. I loved being with Michael last night. "I guess so. After meeting with you I feel motivated to live an active, full and vibrant life, enriched by my own self-love. I embrace my uniqueness and will take more time to walk and move each day. I will focus and be present to life and to all that brings joy. I feel strong and resilient, as well as calm and motivated, to live and love, really love. Thank you, Billy, you are a king. Your wisdom and gifts, I promise to share…"

CHAPTER 11

Perception

Over the next couple of days my thoughts remain on my time up in the High Country resting in Snow Gum Billy. Because of my experience with the previous snow gum at Kosciuszko I had thought Billy's lesson was going to be mostly about overcoming obstacles. I consider this original idea and I realise that it's all about perception. What makes something an obstacle in the first place? Something is only difficult if I label it that way. Everything, of course, is adventure and opportunity. Dropping my phone in the lake has given me a brand-new phone, and the camera in my new mobile phone is incredible. My hair was fixed with no extra charge. I was even gifted a treatment while I relaxed at the salon.

Everything depends on how I view it. Yesterday I got into a car which was nearly out of fuel. Was that a challenge? When I stopped at the very next service station there were beautiful Christmas lilies on sale for half-price, so I bought two bunches.

My life is all about perception. I know Michael and I could have stayed in our swag at the top of the hill. We left as Michael was worried about more stormy weather approaching. Either way, the morning was still mystical and special as I witnessed the rising sun.

Closing my eyes and taking deep heart breaths, I connect back into my friend Snow Gum Billy.

"I'm fairly sure I understand the final lesson and gift I need." I look up at his trunk and branches. He looks like he's flexing his muscles this morning. I smile.

"I'm glad you realised, without me telling you, that your life is how you wish to perceive it. When the snow gum on Mt Kosciuszko told you that he was the tree of obstacles, then that became your focus. Perhaps you expected I would tell you the same thing? Remember that you drove to me up the mountains with ease, and the rain stopped just before you arrived. Everything was great until a little panic set in. That too was fine. Your life is not about obstacles. It is about opportunity, adventure and the invitation to live an abundant life."

I nod my head and gratitude seeps through my being. Life flows when I'm grateful. I feel instantly uplifted, not drained.

"I feel motivated to see my life in this way, not as a series of obstacles," I laugh. "Before I met you, why did I need to meet the snow gum in Kosciuszko?"

"It was part of your journey towards this gift, this lesson. Embrace life and all its adventure. Remember all I've shown you through the reflective messages of my own growth," Snow Gum Billy ends our conversation.

I feel settled, calm and happy. I knew something wasn't complete and now I see I had to realise how important my own perception is.

I place one hand on my heart and the other on one of Snow Gum's big smooth muscly branches. His strength gives me strength.

Today, I promise to be motivated to live life to the full. My life is abundant and it is calling to me. I'm ready for the next adventure.

Also by Rochelle

Banyan Tree Wisdom: My Gift to You
Banyan Tree Wisdom: Wisdom Cards
Meeting Rosie Banyan:
Learning Forgiveness, Trust and Love
I Give You My Word: Journal

EARTH GIANT TREE GIFT SERIES
(GIFT BOOKS & AUDIO BOOKS)

Book 1: Oak Tree's Gift
Book 2: Baobab Tree's Gift
Book 3: Banyan Tree's Gift
Book 4: Rainbow Gum's Gift
Book 5: Olive Tree's Gift
Book 6: Pagoda Tree's Gift
Book 7: Snow Gum Tree's Gift
Book 8: Moreton Bay Fig's Gift

ALCHEMY OILS

Banyan Tree: 'Restore Balance', 'Dream',
'Release' & 'Beauty Wisdom Power'
Oak Tree: 'Truth'
Baobab Tree 'Connection'
Banyan Tree 'Balance'
Rainbow Gum 'Joy'
Olive Tree 'Confidence'
Pagoda Tree 'Clarity'
Snow Gum Tree 'Motivated'
Moreton Bay Fig 'Dreaming'

www.treevoice.global

About the Author

A busy business owner, wife and mother, Rochelle thrived in the corporate and finance world in her early adult years. Then, after her fourth son, a wave of post-natal depression debilitated her, forcing her to re-visit the horrors of her sexually abusive childhood. With grit and determination she laboured against her own broken past and breathed life back into her shutdown heart, cracking open its language and capturing it in writing. She learned to trust in the universal soul path she'd stepped onto.

Each time she experienced a healing method that helped her, Rochelle became qualified in that field to then help others. She became a Bowen Therapist, Reiki and Seichem Master, Clinical Hypnotherapist using NLP methods, Journey Worker and Intuitive Healer. She also owned and ran a Day Spa and Healing Centre in North East Victoria.

Rochelle now immerses herself in connections with nature as they flow, bringing to life the lessons and messages through writing, speaking and facilitating. Her journey has led her to many parts of the globe. She has pitched to Hollywood in New York; she has hosted women's retreats in Bali; she has learned from poverty-stricken leaders in Senegal Africa; and she discovered the 'simple' life in Vanuatu.

Rochelle's message is honest, raw and authentic, and her words are greatly needed as we all navigate our next chapter here on earth.

AUTHOR, SPEAKER, ALCHEMIST,
A LOVER OF NATURE AND
VIBRANT LIVING

Connect with Rochelle

hello@treevoice.global

www.facebook.com/TreeVoiceAuthor

www.facebook.com/RochelleHeverenAuthor

Instagram: @treevoiceglobal

Instagram: @rochelle_with_love_x

www.treevoice.global

www.ingramcontent.com/pod-product-compliance
Lightning Source LLC
Chambersburg PA
CBHW032051290426
44110CB00012B/1037